MOTIVATION

LESSONS FROM THE 3 BEST MOTIVATIONAL SPEAKERS IN THE WORLD. LEARN FROM: TONY ROBBINS, OPRAH WINFREY AND ARNOLD SCHWARZENEGGER

BY

Paul Goleman

Copyright © 2016 by Paul Goleman. All rights reserved.

Without limiting the rights under copyright reserved above no part of this book may be reproduced in any form or by any electronic or mechanical means including information storage and retrieval systems, without permission in writing from the author. The only exception is by a reviewer, who may quote short excerpts in a review.

TABLE OF CONTENTS

Introduction 4

Chapter 1: Motivational Message - Tony Robbins 5

Chapter 2: Motivational Advice - Oprah Winfrey 8

Chapter 3: Motivational Gems - Arnold Schwarzenegger 12

Conclusion 15

Change Your Brain, Change Your Life in 21 days 16

    Introduction 17

    Step I: Change Your Brain with New Resolutions 19

    Step II: Change Your Brain with Optimism 25

    Step III: Change Your Brain with Challenging Skills 31

    Step IV: Change Your Brain with 9 Scientifically Proven Daily Habits 35

    Step V: Change Your Life with a Mentor 39

    Conclusion 41

About Paul Goleman 42

Introduction

Today's rat race has everybody caught up, thereby making motivation seem like a rare commodity to possess. Right from office goers to students, everybody is vying to outdo each other, but often get distracted by things that keep happening around them.

The need of the hour is to, therefore, have a consistent source of motivation that will help people chase their deepest desires. Motivation can be viewed as one of the pre-requisites to availing all that you truly desire. Motivation should be a part and parcel of your everyday life and something that gives you the strength to chase down your goals and ambitions. Without motivation, you will not be able to go after your dreams and you will end up settling for a lackluster, mediocre life.

Motivation can be seen as an inspiration to do better in life - It will help in increasing your ambitions in life.

In this book, we will look at top advice from some of the best motivational speakers in the world, including motivation extraordinaire Tony Robbins, successful entrepreneur Oprah Winfrey, and ex-California governor Arnold Schwarzenegger. The book is meant to help you draw inspiration from these people and improve the different aspects of your life.

Chapter 1: Motivational Message - Tony Robbins

Tony Robbins is a big name in the long list of motivational speakers across the world.

Here is looking at top advice from motivational coach Tony Robbins:

• **"Life is a gift, and it offers us the privilege, opportunity, and responsibility to give something back by becoming more."**

It is important for you to look at your life as a gift that you have to be thankful for and nurture. The best way to remain motivated is to think of all the things that you can do in life and attain the best results. You have to try and tap into every possible opportunity. Many people tend to think that if they pass up on one opportunity then another one will surely come through, but this is the wrong belief to have as it is imperative to try and capitalize on every little opportunity that comes your way.

• **"Successful people ask better questions, and as a result, they get better answers."**

Do not refrain from asking questions as it will not make you any smaller than the other person. It is important to remain motivated, so you can learn about new things. You must remain enthusiastic and ask questions to know more about the various aspects of life. Regardless of whether it is a subordinate or a colleague that you seek the answer from, you must ask questions to ensure that you are in the know of things.

- **"We can change our lives. We can do, have, and be exactly what we wish."**

We are capable of changing our lives regardless of what others say about it. It is not entirely impossible to change the way we look at things or how we behave in certain situations. The idea is to remain motivated enough to look at life from a different perspective. You can change your ideologies and aim higher. You can be exactly who you want to be just by thinking of it and doing the right things to accomplish it.

- **"Lack of emotion causes lack of progress and lack of motivation."**

It is important for us, as humans, to feel emotions on a regular basis. You cannot expect to remain motivated to attain your life's goals if you don't attach emotions towards them. For example, if you wish to lose weight within a short amount of time, it is important for you to get attached to the image of a thinner you in order to successfully lose weight. Similarly, it is vital to seek an emotional attachment when you wish to remain motivated, in order to successfully complete a task.

- **"Most people fail in life because they major in minor things."**

When it comes to going after your goals, there is no point in delving into the minor aspects of life. By doing so, you only end up wasting your own time. It is best to go over all the major aspects of life and forget about the minor things. These can be everyday things that bother you and eat away into your time and energy. If there is a way to avoid it, then you might as well do so or have checks in place to stop you from pondering over trivial thoughts.

- "Where focus goes, energy flows."

Focus and motivation go hand in hand – the higher your focus, the higher your motivation It is extremely important for you to heighten your focus if you wish to heighten your level of motivation. You must be open to the idea of focusing on the important aspects so as to reach your goal sooner.

- "It's what you practice in private that you will be rewarded for in public."

Practice your motivation in private. You don't really have to make a show of how motivated a person you truly are. You can motivate yourself on a daily basis to make it easier to achieve your inner desires.

Chapter 2: Motivational Advice - Oprah Winfrey

Oprah Winfrey is one of the most successful female entrepreneurs in America and is looked up to by millions of people around the world. Oprah is a self-driven and motivated person, who has managed to rise from bad situations and chase down her dreams and desires.

Here are some quotes from Oprah that will inspire you on your journey to remain motivated for life:

• "The reason I've been able to be so financially successful is my focus has never, ever for one minute been money."

This is a very important quote to understand. Here, Oprah stresses on the fact that her inspiration was never just monetary benefits and in fact, wasn't a motivation at all. This can differ from people to people, but it is important to focus on more important things than material desires. If you remain true to your goals and motivated enough to attain the best in life, then other things will automatically follow suit including money. You must not make the end goal the main criterion for your motivation and only look at it as a by-product of attaining your inner desires.

• "The big secret in life is that there is no big secret. Whatever your goal, you can get there if you're willing to work."

There is no one secret that successful people credit their success to. It is a combination of willpower and a need to attain the best in life. If you are willing to put in hard work, then you will surely see results. The more important aspect is to set your –self-goals, remain motivated and go after the desires. It will obviously be easier said than done, but a must if you wish to attain your life's desires.

• **"Create the highest, grandest vision possible for your life because you become what you believe."**

Don't refrain from setting a mental image of your achievements. It is vital that you see yourself, in the future, in a way that you have attained all your goals and desires. You have chased down each of your desires that have led you to attain inner satisfaction. The vision you create in your mind should not be mediocre in nature. If you believe and envision yourself as being the most popular, famous or rich person in the world, then the motivation is bound to empower you.

• **"We can't become what we need to be by remaining what we are."**

It is important for you to reset your goals from time to time. Even if you are the most successful person in the world, it is important to restructure your goals and aim higher. You cannot achieve it all, so you must chase down the next big goal. If you remain satisfied where you are and with what you have, then you will not know what it is like to attain the next big thing.

- **"Passion is energy. Feel the power that comes from focusing on what excites you."**

One key aspect of motivation is remaining excited. It is important for you to be excited about your work and other aspects if you wish to go after your desires. If you feel the passion, then you are sure to progress in life. Set yourself goals that will excite you to put in your best. If you settle for things that are lackluster, then you will find it difficult to achieve your desires. It is important for you to feel a physical urge to go after your desires and fulfill them one by one.

- **"Turn your wounds into wisdom."**

Don't make the mistake of delving into your wounds because they are just stepping stones to your success. You must take away the wisdom that your wounds leave behind and remain motivated regardless of whatever is thrown your way. The biggest motivation that you can have is the need to do better than what you are already doing in life. It is the only thing that will take you forward and prevent you from lapsing.

- **"Surround yourself with only people who are going to lift you higher."**

Remember to always surround yourself with people who are going to help you remain motivated for life. People capable of tapping into your creative and positive side are the ones who will help you attain the best things in life. Although most of us are surrounded by a mixture of people, it is best to try and spend as much time with the positive people and less with negative ones; this way you will remain happy, which will, in turn, increase your motivation.

- **"Breathe. Let go. And remind yourself that this very moment is the only one you know you have for sure."**

One important aspect of remaining motivated is letting go of the past. You must focus on the present and also the future, to a certain extent. If you get carried away and delve into the past, then you will not be able to remain motivated for long.

Chapter 3: Motivational Gems - Arnold Schwarzenegger

Arnold Schwarzenegger is a motivational figure to millions of people around the world. He has managed to go from being a body builder to an actor to a successful politician.

Here is some motivational advice from Schwarzenegger himself:

• **"I'm addicted to exercise and I have to do something every day."**

This is an important lesson to take away from Schwarzenegger. Physical health is extremely important and is essential for you to focus on developing physical strength. It does not matter what type of exercise you take up, as long as it helps in increasing your stamina and keeps your body fit, it will help you remain motivated to chase your life's desires. You can switch it up from time to time to make it interesting.

• **"Training gives us an outlet for suppressed energies created by stress and thus tones the spirit just as exercise conditions the body."**

Stress is now a big part of everybody's life. It is extremely important for you to get rid of the stress and remain as calm as possible. The best way to do so is by exercising on a regular basis and also taking up activities that will calm you down. This can include yoga and tai chi.

- **"I became Mr. Universe; I became a successful businessman. And even though some people say I still speak with a slight accent, I have reached the top of the acting profession."**

Do not be affected by what others say about you or think about you; allowing their thoughts to affect you can affect your motivation. It is up to you to shape your future and what others say is just their opinion and will not change what you are. It is vital for you to think of their words as a mere stepping-stone for you to improve yourself because only then will you be able to attain your life's dreams and desires.

- **"Well, you know, I'm the forever optimist."**

It is essential for you to be a positive person when you wish to attain the best things in life. Optimism coupled with hard work will help you improve your life through several folds. You must focus on building on the positive vibes and letting go of the negative ones. Many people questioned Schwarzenegger's decisions when he wished to become an actor and even a politician, but he managed to remain optimistic and proved all his haters wrong. You must also focus on the positives and clear out the negative aspects of life.

- **"For me, life is continuously being hungry. The meaning of life is not simply to exist, to survive, but to move ahead, to go up, to achieve, to conquer."**

This is one motivational quote that is sure to inspire anybody and everybody. It is important for you to move forward and not get stuck where you are. You must aim higher and try to conquer one milestone after another. After all, you will not know what you are capable of if you don't give it a fair shot!

Conclusion

With these pearls of wisdom from some of the best in the business, we have come to an end to this book. I thank you once again for choosing this book and I hope you have enjoyed reading it.

Remember this - remaining motivated can seem like a tough task; however, it is a must, especially if you wish to achieve the best in life. Motivation comes in different ways in your life; you need to choose what inspires you to do better in life. You can draw inspiration from the advice provided in this book or you can find something that drives you from within to get the much-needed motivation and inspiration in life.

So don't wait anymore, get started with what you've always wanted to do. Follow your heart.

Good luck!

CHANGE YOUR BRAIN, CHANGE YOUR LIFE IN 21 DAYS

A COUPLE OF POWERFUL STEPS TO CREATE THE LIFE THAT YOU DESERVE

Introduction

The human brain is very complex. Scientists have been studying and trying to unveil its power for ages. They believe that the human brain is unbelievably powerful. However, its full capacity and potentials are still unknown. Earlier, scientists used to think that each and every human being is born with a specific pattern of brain capacity and that cannot be changed. A child is born with a specific number of brain cells that remains same till the end of his life.

But, modern science has found evidences that contradict this age old belief.

The brain can and does change throughout a person's life. Plus, the brain is quite adaptive in nature. Scientists call this neuroplasticity. According to new findings, challenging activities can influence a human brain to grow and be more efficient. When you perform the routine day to day tasks, the brain gets used to them and employs same neural pathways to perform the work. But when you expose yourself to new, challenging and unknown tasks or to a problem, the brain tries to accomplish the task or solve the problem by establishing new neural pathways or making new connections between the cells. This overall process improves brain capacity and makes a person more intelligent.

The brain is no different than your body muscles. You grow it through consistent workouts, utmost care, and nourishment. You will have to develop new habits to help your brain grow and get smarter. This book covers a wide range of techniques and lifestyle habits that can change your brain, your intelligence and thus your life. These techniques are target based where you deliberately push the brain to break its limits. In other words, you force your brain to use more than its usual capacity. You can figure out different ways to include these techniques in your lifestyle.

These brain empowering techniques are incredibly easy to incorporate into your day to day life. Some of these techniques are new habits that will take a bit more than usual efforts to develop. But, those habits are potential for your overall brain growth. Some other techniques that you will get to know through this book will be brain challenging activities, like exposing yourself to your biggest fears. Your brain will recognize the situations as a challenge and try hard to figure out ways to stand out.

We need an efficient brain and winning attitude to become an achiever. This book will show how you can transform your brain and attitude to have your dream life.

Let's begin.

STEP I: CHANGE YOUR BRAIN WITH NEW RESOLUTIONS

PRACTICE 5 MOST OVERLOOKED MORNING RITUALS TO CHANGE YOUR BRAIN IN 21 DAYS

"Successful people aren't born that way. They become successful by establishing the habit of doing things unsuccessful people don't like to do. The successful people don't always like doing these things themselves; they just get on and do them.... By Don Marquis

Why are some people more successful than others? Why some people appear to be effortlessly efficient in managing problems, making new social relationships, initiating good conversations, influencing people and producing great results? Are successful people born with a distinctive mindset and excellent brainpower?

First, we should understand that apart from few exceptional cases, successful and happy people are not always blessed to have a convenient life. They are not always born with luxuries. Predominantly, they build their dreams and life on their own.

The primary aspects that differentiate successful people from the average are: their perspectives, mindset, and emotional intelligence. Successful and happy people are mentally strong, highly optimistic, determined and goal oriented people. Their extraordinary enthusiasm and aspiration make them inspiring and influential.

If you are good in mathematics, that indicates you have a good logical intelligence. It will also be considered that you have a strong problem-solving skill. But, unless you are after academic excellence, your mathematical skill alone will not ensure that you will be happy and have an excellent life.

To achieve success and happiness, you need an enthusiastic, logical and emotionally intelligent mind. A strong emotional intelligence can exceptionally improve a person's life. Emotional intelligence is referred to a person's ability to identify, control and manage various kinds of emotional aspects empathetically. Especially, your ability to control your negative emotions, like sadness, anxiety and anger, can make your life simple and successful. Your emotional response during the critical moments can influence your decisions and actions. For example, you live with a person who often criticizes you for your shortcomings and make harsh judgements. You feel bad. Now, if you take the person's consistent negative remarks personally and too seriously, you will likely lose your mind, be mad at him and indulge in a direct fight. It will make you stressed and your life will be even more critical.

But, if you can develop resilience and strong emotional intelligence, the person's behaviour and judgements will never negatively influence your emotions. You will be strong to take no judgements and criticism personally and only concentrate on your life and ambitions. No external stimuli will be able to divert you from your ambitions. However, if you are too emotional and have a very negative mindset, this will take a lot of practice and long-term commitment to a systematic approach of self-development and growth. You will need to improve your focus and change your mind set to evolve your thoughts and perspectives.

Do not worry. Brain training for a strong emotional intelligence is a gradual process. So let's take one step at a time. The remaining chapters of this book will explain how we need to change our brain to be happy, confident, influential and successful in our life.

First, we will learn how to start brain training with new resolutions. To change your brain and mindset, you will need to force it to adapt new habits and challenges. Choose a day and start your brain training with these 5 powerful morning rituals.

1. Force Yourself to Be an Early Riser: This will be an excellent step for lifestyle improvement and challenging the mind. By waking up early in the morning, you will have extra time to visualize the goals of the day, prioritize your tasks, and most importantly, some more time for self-care. You can just sit still, close your eyes and do nothing for a moment. Or you can go out and enjoy the stunning and spectacular view of the early morning. You can have quality time free from all external interruptions. So you can actually use this time for the task that you presume to be the most important and valuable for you at present.

2. Meditate for 20 Minutes: To be accurate, brain training starts when you consciously detach your mind from the ongoing negative self-talks and re-engage into the useful positive thoughts. To achieve excellence, you need a calm mind, a clear thought process, a positive outlook, confidence and courage for consistent improvement.

Meditation is a scientifically proven brain training tool. So if you are thinking of improving your emotional intelligence, practice meditation long term. Meditation is proven to improve the section of the brain that is responsible for logical thinking. Also, it disengages the section of the brain that triggers emotions like anger, sadness and other negative responses. The technique of meditation is extremely helpful for calming the mind, increasing self-awareness and improving attention. When you practice it for a long time, you become aware of your own thoughts, strengths and start to identify scope for improvements. Self-awareness is very important for improving the quality of life, understand the opportunities and areas of success. So, the best time to practice meditation can be early morning. Make this an indispensable part of your daily morning rituals.

3. Get Some Sun Exposure: According to medical science, sunlight exposure can trigger the release of serotonin hormone in the brain. Serotonin hormone is responsible for arousing feelings like happiness and satisfaction. It can be an excellent natural alternative cure for problems like mood disorder and depression. Therefore, a moderate amount of sunlight exposure must be a part of your daily morning rituals. Sunlight is also an excellent natural source of vitamin Did you know that lack of vitamin D and depression has a direct relation? Unfortunately, depression, if remains unidentified and unaddressed, can become a major trouble for your life and professional growth. Although depression is a biological disease, this issue should be taken care of as quickly as possible. So why not use the early morning hours to give yourself a little sun exposure and boost your emotional response?

4. Eat At Least 30 Grams of Protein: Include about 30 grams of protein in your daily breakfast. Protein is considered an essential brain food. Lack of protein can devastatingly affect your thought process and mental clarity. Why? It is pure science. Protein is one of the most important component found in the brain chemicals called neurotransmitters. These neurotransmitters are responsible for exchanging information in your brain and also for triggering different types of emotions. So, for the overall nourishment of the important neurotransmitters and brain cells, you need a reasonable amount of protein intake. Hormones are basically protein. So, if you do not maintain protein balance, the brain hormones will go crazy and make you feel depressed and overwhelmed. This will certainly affect your intelligence, concentration, and focus. So, to change your brain and improve overall emotional intelligence, you also need to think about your brain health and its nourishment.

5. Read and Write: Another efficient way to improve your brain health can be engaging the mind into reading and writing. But, include these activities in your early morning rituals for efficient results. Reading and writing are excellent for improving brain's cognitive functions. In addition, writing improves critical thinking process and makes your brain more analytical. Writing is also a very powerful tool for improving mental health as it allows freedom of expression. When you write, you pen down all your thoughts and opinions without the fear of being judged or criticized. The freedom of expression and free flow of feelings improve mental health and thus your mindset and important brain functions.

If you are a night owl, you will feel waking up early morning next to impossible. So try to continue the same schedule for at least couple of weeks. Continue these morning rituals for 21 days. In addition, you will have to practice few exercises to protect your mind from toxic influences. These defence mechanisms will build a shield against negativity so that you can free your mind from unwanted interruptions and only concentrate on incorporating positive transformations. Check out the next chapter to learn the art of brain positivity.

STEP II: CHANGE YOUR BRAIN WITH OPTIMISM

"The battle you are going through is not fueled by the words or actions of others; it is fueled by the mind that gives it importance." — Shannon L. Alder

Lack of focus, optimism, enthusiasm and emotional intelligence can distant you from each and every possibilities of success. Thus, you will have to build a strong personality and a powerful brain that no external factors except your own passion and drive can influence.

In this chapter, we will be talking about building mind positivity to overcome the common barriers to success. We will particularly talk about how oversensitivity, in the absence of emotional intelligence, can make your life difficult, and how you should change your brain to overcome this problem.

Oversensitivity can become a trouble maker for your life, especially if you are expecting life simplicity, success and happiness. During some unexpected events or situations, oversensitive people quickly hold onto a certain type of emotion and continue to suffer mentally for a very long time. Some of the noticeable signs of oversensitivity are:

• Fear of criticism. For example, the thought of being criticized is so horrible to you that you go to any extent to avoid criticism and work hard to please people. This approach can be mentally exhausting.

• Taking too much time for a decision. You fear of being blamed for taking a wrong decision. You become too conscious and reluctant to take any risk.

• Quick and strong reactions to unwanted situations.

• Poor pain tolerance ability. An oversensitive person feels any kind of pain, triggering from injuries, normal headache, and muscle pain, stronger than the others.

• You are easily scared.

• Hating bright lights, noises or loud voice.

• Thinking too much. During critical moments, do you tend to be swept by your own thoughts so much that you forget to take a right action?

• The tendency of taking the impact of bad decisions strongly.

• Oversensitive people often prefer to be a lone wolf.

However, oversensitive people are also found to be great at teamwork. So everything about oversensitivity is not bad. But, if you fail to control this specific emotional aspect, it can become a potential barrier to success. You will feel overwhelmed, become hesitant to take risks and might easily turn into a pessimistic person. It is important to note that people can use your oversensitive nature to manipulate your behavior, actions and most important decisions of life. So how do you fight back oversensitivity, negativism and toxic influences?

Let's first understand how the brain works when you feel oversensitive.

Scientists have long confirmed that oversensitivity is a neurological process and not any personality trait. If a person is shy, too empathetic or emotional, that is mostly because of the person's genetic feature. Scientist Elaine Aron have recently confirmed this fact. The section in the brain which is responsible for creating feelings, awareness, empathy, integration of sensory information has been found to be more active in oversensitive people in comparison to the low sensitive people.

There is no harm in being oversensitive if you know how to not let others take advantage of your emotions, or you can make yourself calm, creative, optimistic, safe and happy during the most difficult situations. Learn to suppress oversensitivity to allow your strengths grow. Here are few things that you can do.

Practice these 5 defence techniques to change your brain and use oversensitivity to your advantage.

1. Accept Oversensitivity: Do not try to hide your sensitive emotional responses. Accept that you are an oversensitive person and there is nothing wrong about it. Accept that it is part of your identity. If others try to tag you as a shy and introverted person, tell them this is what you are. Do not feel ashamed of yourself. If you do not feel confident about yourself, it will downgrade your self-esteem. If you accept oversensitivity and try to understand your emotions, you will never feel the urge of changing yourself and feel that you are no less than the others. So the first and most important thing to do is that you accept yourself and feel good about yourself.

2. Increase Self-awareness: Understand your over sensitiveness. Practice self-awareness to understand the triggers. There are some particular situations, moments, or factors that force you to react too strong. Understand what those factors are. Practicing self-awareness can be extremely helpful for making the mind silent and improving your focus. You will need a calm and relaxed mind to understand the different aspects that influence your emotions and behavior. Practice mindfulness or meditation to improve self-awareness. Meditation will improve your attention. With a strong attention and mind focus, you will be able to find your strengths. You can then use your strengths to fight back situations that make you overwhelmed. That way you will learn to control your immediate emotional reactions in response to a situation. You will be able to keep a track of your actions and behaviors at a certain moment.

3. Invite More Criticism: Throw yourself to situations that you consider most uncomfortable. For example, if you hate criticism, do not hide from it. Instead, take criticism positively. Your brain is a powerful adaptive tool. So train your brain to respond positively to negative situations. Remember that there will always be some people who love criticism. But, you have to change your perspective. Do not think that criticism is mental exhausting. Sometimes, you can learn a lot from criticism. You may learn about the things that need improvements. You should take criticism as a tool for personal evaluation. It will help you understand where you need to improve yourself and how you can do so.

4. Learn to Manage Reactions: Understand that you do not need to react to everything that come your way. Life cannot be same all the time. There will some good as well as bad moments. You cannot predict everything. You cannot control everything. So, accept that you do not need to identify yourself with everything happening in your life. Yes, you are part of everything that surrounds your life. But sometimes, things get better when you learn to let go. So try not to be too reactive to every situations or incidents of life. If something makes you happy, enjoy the moment. If something unexpected or unwanted happens, accept it and move on. Your mind will help you build resilience. Do not stick to any particular emotion for a long time. Get rid of negative emotions as they can drain your energy.

5. Choose Your Associations Wisely: Many accomplished entrepreneurs believe that our friends and company deeply influence our thoughts, actions, and decisions of life. So, try to stay away from pessimists at any cost. You do not need people around who resist growth and discourage ambition. Try to be with people who inspire you. Psychologists believe in the principles of law of attraction. It has been seen that people who have high-level education love to associate with people with an elite education background. Religious people often associate with people of faith. Physically fit people often enjoy the association of people who are also fit. So, for mind positivity, choose your friends wisely.

The brain is exactly like your body muscles. It grows as you workout and nourish with utmost care. But we often neglect its wellness and expose the brain to stress consistently. Your brain is naturally designed to anticipate threats and prepare you for possible dangers. But, do not get overwhelmed with the process of anticipation. You also need to identify the potentials of your brain and use them for improving your life and increase chances of success. The next chapter explains the key skills that can engage your mind a productive way and increase its efficiency.

STEP III: CHANGE YOUR BRAIN WITH CHALLENGING SKILLS

Your brain will evolve if you expose it to challenges. Brain science has discovered that cognitive and social engagements can help us achieve clarity of thoughts, keep us mentally sharp and more energetic even during the older age. This happens because of brain's natural ability to grow new cells and establish new connections between the cells. Scientists address this process as neuronal plasticity.

Therefore, one of the essential aspects that can help you build a positive mind and confidence is your social skill. Besides improving your thinking skill, social skills also help to build a strong emotional intelligence.

Social skills are primarily the interpersonal skills that make you more efficient in interacting with people who you know or may not know. If you can practice these social skills, you will gradually develop a more empathetic mindset and be more efficient in controlling your emotions. These skills will help you achieve mental clarity and gain confidence. So here are the things that you should practice to change your brain:

1. Communication Skills: To build a strong emotional intelligence and a powerful mind, you have to spend more time in developing an influential communication skill. Communication skill includes your verbal ability, writing skill and also your listening skill. You should be able to clearly communicate your opinions and share your views during social engagements. Also, concentrate on building a strong writing skill. Writing needs a person to think rationally. In addition, creative writing improves a person's imagination ability. The overall process will make you more analytical and highly efficient in communication.

You can also practice communication skill by participating more in group events, conferences, workshops and other informal social gatherings. The ultimate goal is to challenge the mind to understand different types of situations, comprehend emotions of other people and become better at persuasive exchange of information.

2. Leadership Skills: Developing leadership skills is not easy either. You do not have to be a perfect leader. But, you can challenge yourself to develop at least some of the leadership qualities if not all. Leaders are inspirational, great problem solvers, innovative, honest, self-motivated, have excellent communication skill and build relationships. To build all or some of these skills, you will need a focused mind, determination, resilience and consistency. You have to expose yourself to uncertainties. You have to get out of your comfort zone. For example, if you are not good at public speaking, participate more in group discussions, conferences and presentations. You have to try consistently until you gain confidence and overcome the fear of public speaking. Remember that your brain loves challenges. The more you throw problems at it, powerful and smarter it gets.

3. Persuasion Skill: Likewise, persuasion skill can also force your brain to evolve. Persuasion skill needs an understanding of psychology and human behavior. Your persuasion skill can make you influential. However, this skill is highly complex in nature as your brain has to develop strategies to influence human thoughts and behavior. Take this challenge to put your brain in more critical atmospheres. Have fun. Do not stress yourself if you are not able to succeed. Your aim is not becoming a perfect influencer but to master the art of problem-solving. You will have to make your brain ready to accept challenges.

4. Time Management Skill: We know that time management is one of the biggest challenges. So why not try to master the skill? Try to use your time efficiently. Target to improve every day. Find out ways to manage more number of tasks in a short time. For example, you usually take 30 mints to spend 140 calories in the gym. So, next time when you hit the gym, target to spend 140 calories in 20 mints. But this is an example. You can challenge yourself every day to accomplish any tasks in time efficient ways. You need to challenge your brain to complete a task more efficiently and in a short time.

5. Join Online Brain Challenging Programs: We should cherish the fact that modern technology has brought us numbers of easy means for self-growth and development. For example, there are some amazing websites like lumosity.com and brainhq.com that can help you improve cognitive functions. Or you can also take a digital photography training to improve your brain. These brain-engaging activities are scientifically proven to be highly effective for cognitive enhancement. This means a consistent involvement in these types of activities can be beneficial for improving your memory, thinking ability, attention, learning and reading skills.

If a situation appears to be more difficult than you can imagine, you should slow down. During the difficult moments, try not to react immediately. Instead, take some time to understand the severity of the problem. Learn to relax and take the time to gradually evolve. Consistency is more important than anything else. So, you must try to follow and stick to all brain improvement techniques suggested in this book for at least 21 days. The chapter below explains the activities that you must incorporate in your daily life to improve your brain capacity and change your life.

STEP IV: CHANGE YOUR BRAIN WITH 9 SCIENTIFICALLY PROVEN DAILY HABITS

Brain workouts are also important. Many simple daily habits can make your brain smarter and efficient. Here are few of them:

1. Start Your Day After 7 Hours of Sleep: You need enough sleep to rewire your brain. Do not listen to people who criticize you for your extended sleep duration. Sleep deprivation is a weapon of destruction for your overall health. If you usually sleep for 6 hours during the weekdays, try to sleep for an extra hour or so during the weekends. It will make you feel mentally sharp and energetic.

2. Deep Breathe: Scientists have long proved that controlled breathing can influence your brain size. The technique can actually improve the sections of the brain that are responsible for critical thinking, reasoning, memory and attention. When you deep breathe, you consciously try to control your breathing pattern. This process improves self-awareness. Exercises like Yoga and meditation are especially very helpful. So, practice deep breathing once you wake up. Make it your daily habit.

3. Practice Gratitude and Affirmation: Practice gratitude to increase your mental well-being. Take 2 minutes to sit in a silent place, close your eyes and try to recall relevant things of your life. Show gratitude to beautiful and most precious things of your life. Be thankful to have a supporting family, or being able to fulfill your own dreams.

Affirmations will help you bring focus on your goals and positive intentions. When you wake up, close your eyes and say "I am a good human being". "I help people". "I work excellent". These affirmations will improve mind positivity.

4. Lift Weights: Strength training is also important for brain change. If you want mental clarity, a sharp and intelligent mind, you should hit the gym and try strength training couple of times in a week. Yes, strength training offsets the impact of stress on the brain. In addition, it promotes brain growth.

5. Try these Brain Exercises: Different day to day life activities like cooking, trying to recall the events of last two days, learning a music instrument and a foreign language, knitting, painting, solving puzzles, etc. are considered excellent brain enhancement exercises. Practice few of these things whenever you have some free time in a day.

6. Read Thought-Provoking Books: You should read books which can challenge your visualization ability and force you to think. Some great books can be "Thinking, Fast and Slow" written by Daniel Kahneman, "This Will Make You Smarter" from the author John Brockman and "If on a winter's night, a traveler" written by Italo Calvino. There are many other amazing books like this. All these books will need you to read attentively and improve your motor skills.

7. Engage into Brain Exhausting Activities: Do things which you think is mentally exhausting for you. If you think practicing mathematics make you mentally tired, this is what you should do more. That is what you need to change your brain and your life. Mentally exhausting activities can be anything which can force you to think and solve a problem. These activities will improve you mental health and your emotional intelligence.

8. Practice Guided Meditation: Meditation can be extremely challenging in the beginning. Telling a wandering mind to focus on a specific thought is almost near to impossible. But, remember that you do not have to perform meditation with acute precision to change your brain. Meditation is a brain training process. When you deliberately try to shift the focus from one thought to another, it increases self-awareness. It helps you understand your own thoughts and let you decide where you would like to focus instead. Try guided meditation to train your brain to focus on imageries of your choice. Set aside 20 minutes of time from your daily schedule to do meditation.

9. Write By Hand: Another excellent way to train the brain is writing by hand. Try to write every morning. Morning is the time when we have the highest willpower and creativity.

The strategic and technical approach mentioned above are very practical and brain empowering. To help your brain evolve and grow, you will have to force it use its maximum capacity. According to science, smart people have the best brain wiring. This means that smart people can efficiently connect the various segments of the brain. But, you can do that as well. Human intelligence is infinite. The more you practice and train the brain through intelligence improving activities, the smarter your brain becomes. An additional recommendation could be taking help from the mentors. The next chapter of the book provides a brief on this aspect.

STEP V: CHANGE YOUR LIFE WITH A MENTOR

Sometimes it becomes very hard for us to keep the motivation on all the time. Sometimes we feel lost and lose directions. That time we need someone who can guide and direct us throughout. Someone who can tell us where we are going wrong.

This is when you need to listen to the experts. For example, Brian Tracy is a self-development expert who trains individuals, professionals, entrepreneurs and businessmen about the various aspects of life development. You need help from such experts. Mentors will help you with their knowledge and experience. A mentor can help you:

• Find your goal. What do you want to achieve in your life? Can you visualize your goal clearly?

• We do not always understand where to find our inspiration. A mentor can help us with that. A mentor can help you understand your own needs and aspirations. When you look for ways to learn more about your dream and aspiration, you find out ways to inspire yourself.

• A mentor can encourage you to continue your journey when you feel demotivated.

• You need a mentor for self-evaluation. If you are trying everything to improve your life, do you really think all your efforts have really made you a different person altogether? Do you notice any improvement in your personality, mindset and perspectives? Your mentor will be able to correctly analyze that and recommend your next course of actions.

•A mentor will help you save time through constant monitoring of improvements and redefining the whole strategies if you are not.

• An excellent mentor can actually change your life overall by pushing you all the way to your goals and ambitions.

People who have mentors reach their goals more often than people who don't.

Conclusion

To make an amazing change in your life, you need to get yourself all the right resources. This book explains some very specific and practical techniques that you must incorporate in your daily life. These techniques will inspire you to take challenges and fight for your dream. Also, always remember that you will have to expose yourself to difficulties and problems to change your brain and your life. Success cannot be achieved through easy means. So, you will have to build a mind that can welcome challenges of life anytime and help you overcome them. In the end, consistency will also matter.

So start your brain training right now.

About Paul Goleman

I'm an entrepreneur, internet marketer, author, life coach, professional speaker, fitness enthusiast, and world traveller. I feel extremely blessed for the life that I live.

I bring 7 years of niche expertise in self-help and personal development. I'm a business management graduate and I like to study people who appear to be unbeatable against all oddities or challenges of life. I seek answers for failures, lack of growth and thus I want to help people reinvent themselves. I believe: Each and every person is the sole controller of his/her life. If you do not take an utmost care of your life, no one else will.

ONE LAST THING...

If you enjoyed this book or found it useful I'd be very grateful if you'd post a short review on Amazon. Your support really does make a difference and I read all the reviews personally so I can get your feedback and make this book even better.

Thanks again for your support!

Made in the USA
Monee, IL
07 November 2019